AIRPLANES

LORI DITTMER

CREATIVE EDUCATION • CREATIVE PAPERBACKS

CONT

ENTS

I AM AN AIRPLANE.

I fly through the sky.

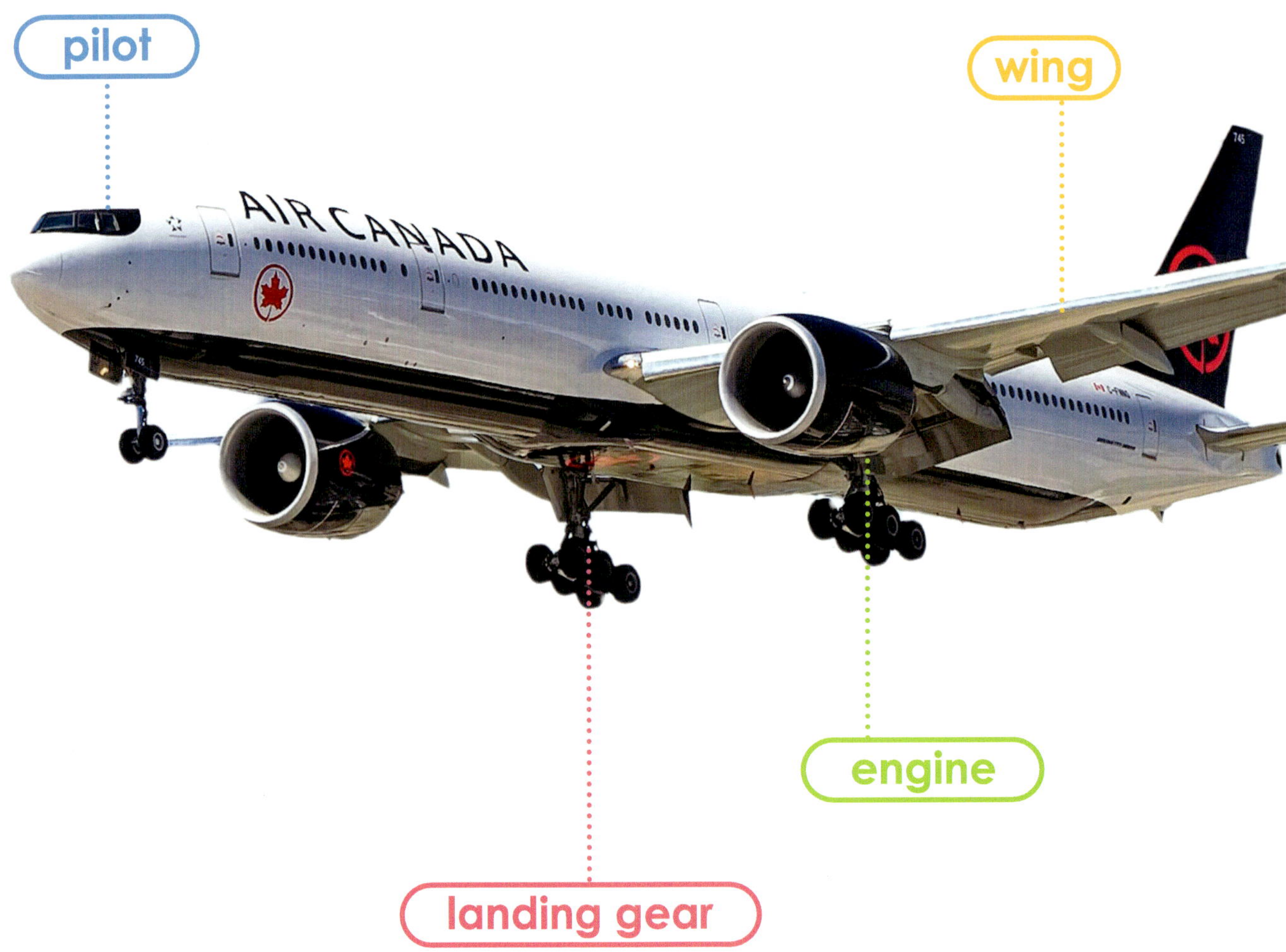

Look at
my wings
and tail!
VN2S-5
N55869
U.S.NAVY
245
245

I carry people and cargo from place to place.

The pilot drives. A co-pilot helps. They sit in the cockpit.

My wheels roll on the runway.
Then I lift my nose. Up, up I go!
Two big engines help me go fast.

I can go more than 500 miles (805 km) per hour!

The pilot finds
the runway.

My wheels touch the ground. Whoosh! We come to a stop.

My job is done!

MAKE A NOISE

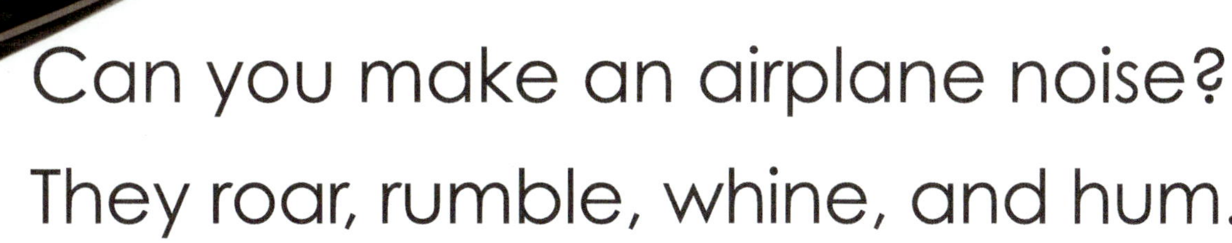

Can you make an airplane noise? They roar, rumble, whine, and hum.

Listen to these sounds:

AIRPLANE WORDS

Cargo: Goods carried by a vehicle

Cockpit: The place where an airplane pilot sits

Engine: A machine that provides power and makes something move

Runway: A smooth strip of ground for airplanes to take off and land

READING CORNER

Dieker, Wendy Strobel. *Airplanes*. Mankato, Minn.: Amicus, 2020.

Harris, Bizzy. *Firefighting Planes*. Minneapolis: Jump!, 2022.

Zobel, Derek. *Airplanes*. Minneapolis: Bellwether Media, 2021.

INDEX

PUBLISHED BY CREATIVE EDUCATION AND CREATIVE PAPERBACKS
P.O. Box 227, Mankato, Minnesota 56002
Creative Education and Creative Paperbacks are imprints of The Creative Company
www.thecreativecompany.us

LIBRARY OF CONGRESS CATALOGING-IN-PUBLICATION DATA
Names: Dittmer, Lori author
Title: Airplanes / Lori Dittmer.
Description: Mankato, Minnesota : Creative Education and Creative Paperbacks, [2026] | Series: Starting out | Includes bibliographical references and index. | Audience: Ages 4-7 | Audience: Grades K-1 | Summary: "Introduce beginning readers to a day in the skies with an airplane in this STEM starter. Includes photos, a labeled vehicle diagram, 'Make a Noise' section, glossary, and further resources"— Provided by publisher.
Identifiers: LCCN 2025013142 (print) | LCCN 2025013143 (ebook) | ISBN 9798895810248 library binding | ISBN 9781682779774 paperback | ISBN 9798895811504 ebook
Subjects: LCSH: Airplanes"—Juvenile literature | CYAC: Airplanes
Classification: LCC TL547 .D5445 2026 (print) | LCC TL547 (ebook) | DDC 629.133/34"— dc23/eng/20250424
LC record available at https://lccn.loc.gov/2025013142
LC ebook record available at https://lccn.loc.gov/2025013143

DESIGN AND PRODUCTION
Design by Rhea Magaro
Art direction by Tom Morgan

PHOTOGRAPHS BY
Dreamstime/Robwilson39, 11, 12–13; Pexels/Pascal Borener, 14, Pieter van der Sandt, cover, Pixabay, 5, Selvin Esteban, 2, Rafael Cosquiere, 7; Unsplash/Chris Leipelt, 6, John McArthur, 4, Josue Isai Ramos Figueroa, 10, Leio McLaren, 9; Wikimedia Commons/MSgt John Nimmo Sr., 8

Printed in the United States